ASP Prep Book 2018-2019
ASP Practice Test Questions for the Association of Safety Professionals Exam

Copyright © 2018 by Trivium Test Prep

ALL RIGHTS RESERVED. By purchase of this book, you have been licensed one copy for personal use only. No part of this work may be reproduced, redistributed, or used in any form or by any means without prior written permission of the publisher and copyright owner.

Trivium Test Prep is not affiliated with or endorsed by any testing organization and does not own or claim ownership of any trademarks, specifically for the ASP exam. All test names (and their acronyms) are trademarks of their respective owners. This study guide is for general information and does not claim endorsement by any third party.

Printed in the United States of America.

TABLE OF CONTENTS

INTRODUCTION to the Associate Safety Professional Exam………………………………1

OVERVIEW of the examination process………………………………………………………4

Preparation and Building your Test Prep Strategy…………………………………………...4

The ASP Body of Knowledge…………………………………………………………………5
DOMAIN 1. RECOGNIZING SAFETY, HEALTH, AND ENVIRONMENTAL HAZARDS 35.4% of the test
Topic 1. Biological Hazards……………………………………………………………...5
Topic 2. Chemical Hazards………………………………………………………………5
Topic 3. Electrical Hazards………………………………………………………………7
Topic 4. Natural Hazards…………………………………………………………………8
Topic 5. Radiation Hazards………………………………………………………………9
Topic 6. Structural and Mechanical Hazards…………………………………………...10
Topic 7. Hazards Related to Fires and Explosions……………………………………..11
Topic 8. Hazards Related to Human Factors and Ergonomics…………………………12

DOMAIN 2. MEASURING, EVALUATING, AND CONTROLLING SAFETY, HEALTH, AND ENVIRONMENTAL HAZARDS
30.9% of the test
Topic 1. Measurement and Monitoring………………………………………………...14
Topic 2. Engineering Controls…………………………………………………………17
Topic 3. Administrative Controls………………………………………………………23
Topic 4. Personal Protective Equipment……………………………………………….28

DOMAIN 3. SAFETY, HEALTH, AND ENVIRONMENTAL TRAINING AND MANAGEMENT 20.6% of the test
Topic 1. Training and Communication Methods……………………………………….30
Topic 2. Management Processes………………………………………………………..32
Topic 3. Inspections and Auditing……………………………………………………...33
Topic 4. Group Dynamics………………………………………………………………34
Topic 5. Project Management…………………………………………………………..35
Topic 6. Risk Management……………………………………………………………..36
Topic 7. Safety, Health, and Environmental Management Systems……………………37

DOMAIN 4. BUSINESS PRINCIPLES, PRACTICES, AND METRICS IN SAFETY, HEALTH, AND ENVIRONMENTAL PRACTICE
13.1% percent of the test
Topic 1. Basic Financial Principles……………………………………………………..38
Topic 2. Probability and Statistics……………………………………………………...39
Topic 3. Performance Metrics and Indicators…………………………………………..41
Final Words and Tips for the test and Sample Questions……………………………...43

Introduction

Congratulations on your decision to pursue the Associate Safety Professional (ASP) designation!

Your decision will have significant impact on the course of your career as a safety professional. The Associate Safety Professional (ASP) designation is one of the premier certifications a safety, occupational health, or industrial hygiene professional can add to their professional portfolio.

This guide will provide you with a quick and informative resource of what one may expect on the ASP exam.

The "Associate Safety Professional" (ASP) and "Certified Safety Professional" (CSP) are registered certification marks issued to the Office to the Board of Certified Safety Professionals.

The Board of Certified Safety Professionals (BCSP) web site at is available at www.bcsp.org

Associate Certified Safety Professionals have several tangible benefits: They earn the respect of other safety professionals. The credentials are often preferred or required by many employers of safety professionals. Many times certification may be required in many government and private contracts. Enhance your level of pay on the average about $24,000 in safety professional salary surveys more per year than safety professionals without certification.

The Board of Certified Safety Professionals defines safety professionals by the following definitions, it is important to understand the classifications and requirements thereof:

"A **Safety Professional** is one who applies the expertise gained from a study of safety science, principles, practices, and other subjects and from professional safety experience to create or develop procedures, processes, standards, specifications, and systems to achieve optimal control or reduction of the hazards and exposures that may harm people, property, or the environment."

"A **Certified Safety Professional** is a safety professional who has met and continues to meet all requirements established by BCSP and is authorized by BCSP to use the Certified Safety Professional title and the CSP credential."

"An **Associate Safety Professional** is a temporary designation awarded by BCSP. This designation describes an individual who has met the academic requirements for the CSP credential and has passed the Safety Fundamentals examination, the first of two examinations leading to the CSP credential."

The ASP Process - The process of earning the interim Associate Safety Professional (ASP) designation is as follows.

1. **Complete and submit the required application materials.** The BCSP will review your application materials to determine whether you have met the academic and experience requirements and are eligible for the Safety Fundamentals examination.

You must have documented experience as defined by the BCSP "Professional safety experience must be the primary function of a position and account for at least 50% of the position's responsibility. Professional safety experience involves analysis, synthesis, investigation, evaluation, research, planning, design, administration, and consultation to the satisfaction of peers, employers, and clients in the prevention of harm to people, property, and the environment. Professional safety experience differs from nonprofessional safety experience in the degree of responsible charge and the ability to defend analytical approaches and recommendations for engineering or administrative controls."

2. **Register to take the Safety Fundamentals examination leading to the interim ASP designation.**
After you register and pay for a Safety Fundamentals examination authorization, BCSP will (1) notify the examination delivery service provider that you are an authorized Safety Fundamentals examination candidate and (2) inform you how long you have to make an appointment and to complete the Safety Fundamentals examination.

3. **Make an appointment to take your examination at a test center.** Your examination will be delivered to you on a computer at your requested test center. You will receive your unofficial result as soon as you log off the test center's computer system. **BCSP will send you your official result within three weeks after you take your examination.**

4. **Complete all requirements for the ASP credential.** After completing all of the requirements, BCSP will award you interim use of the Associate Safety Professional (ASP)
designation.

5. The ASP Credential is awarded to ASPs who subsequently pass the Comprehensive Practice examination and meet the requirements to achieve and retain the credential.

Think about the CSP as the next step in your professional safety career.

Strategy

The Safety Fundamentals examination contains 200 multiple-choice items with four possible answers. You will have five hours to complete the Safety Fundamentals examination.

Use the most appropriate methods to prepare for the Safety Fundamentals examination for your learning style, experience, and memory retention level. This may be a combination of individual study including flashcards, notes pages, this manual and personal notes. Remember, a significant portion of the test will be conveying your knowledge of common practices you use daily in the safety field.

The best way to know how to study is to know where your strengths and weaknesses exist. Each question will contain four parts, each question is scored so guess intelligently and read carefully. Manage your time appropriately. You have five hours for the exam answer those you can answer quickly. Then go back to items that were difficult for you or required considerable time to read, analyze, or compute. After you have gone through the examination once or if you are running out of time, look for items that you have not answered. Draw on your experience and on professional and study references in your own library, a company, or a public library.

In order to tell where you need to apply your preparation efforts score yourself on your level of knowledge for each subject area. The general topics are listed. The evaluation worksheet is adapted from the BCSP self-evaluation you should rate your level of knowledge on each domain and topic included on the Safety Fundamentals examination by circling each area as H = High, M = Medium, or L = Low. This will help you to develop your strategy for effective studying.

Where do you stand?

DOMAIN 1.
RECOGNIZING SAFETY, HEALTH, AND ENVIRONMENTAL HAZARDS

Domain topics Rank your current knowledge High, Medium or Low	H, M or L
Topic 1. Biological Hazards	☐ ☐ ☐
Topic 2. Chemical Hazards	☐ ☐ ☐
Topic 3. Electrical Hazards	☐ ☐ ☐
Topic 4. Natural Hazards	☐ ☐ ☐
Topic 5. Radiation Hazards	☐ ☐ ☐
Topic 6. Structural and Mechanical Hazards	☐ ☐ ☐
Topic 7. Hazards Related to Fires and Explosions	☐ ☐ ☐
Topic 8. Hazards Related to Human Factors and Ergonomics	☐ ☐ ☐

DOMAIN 2.
MEASURING, EVALUATING, AND CONTROLLING SAFETY, HEALTH, AND
ENVIRONMENTAL HAZARDS

Domain topics Rank your current knowledge High, Medium or Low	H, M or L
Topic 1. Measurement and Monitoring	☐ ☐ ☐
Topic 2. Engineering Controls	☐ ☐ ☐
Topic 3. Administrative Controls	☐ ☐ ☐
Topic 4. Personal Protective Equipment	☐ ☐ ☐

DOMAIN 3.
SAFETY, HEALTH, AND ENVIRONMENTAL TRAINING AND MANAGEMENT

Domain topics — Rank your current knowledge High, Medium or Low	H, M or L
Topic 1. Training and Communication Methods	☐ ☐ ☐
Topic 2. Management Processes	☐ ☐ ☐
Topic 3. Inspections and Auditing	☐ ☐ ☐
Topic 4. Group Dynamics	☐ ☐ ☐
Topic 5. Project Management	☐ ☐ ☐
Topic 6. Risk Management	☐ ☐ ☐
Topic 7. Safety, Health, and Environmental Management Systems	☐ ☐ ☐

DOMAIN 4.
BUSINESS PRINCIPLES, PRACTICES, AND METRICS IN SAFETY, HEALTH, AND ENVIRONMENTAL PRACTICE

Domain topics — Rank your current knowledge High, Medium or Low	H, M or L
Topic 1. Basic Financial Principles	☐ ☐ ☐
Topic 2. Probability and Statistics	☐ ☐ ☐
Topic 3. Performance Metrics and Indicators	☐ ☐ ☐

Safety Fundamentals Examination Domain 1
Recognizing Safety, Health, and Environmental Hazards 35.4%

Domain 1 covers 35.4% of the test content

Topic 1 - Biological Hazards

What you need to know: biological hazards are those which include exposures that are commonly associated with working with animals, people, or infectious plant materials. This includes but is not limited to blood and body fluids, plants, insects, bacteria, fungi, mold, viruses and animal excrement or droppings. Biological hazards can be encountered in any work environment such as work in schools, colleges and universities, hospitals, day care facilities, laboratories, emergency response, nursing homes, and outdoor work occupations.

Biological agents have the ability to adversely affect human health in a variety of ways which range from relatively mild, allergic reactions to serious medical conditions, even death. Biological agents are common and widespread in the natural environment and are found in water, soil, plants, and animals. Microbes reproduce rapidly and require minimal resources for survival and as such they are a potential danger in a wide variety of occupational settings.

The most common biological agents the associate safety professional will provide administrative and engineering controls for are anthrax, avian, flu, blood borne pathogens, botulism, foodborne pathogens, Legionnaires' Disease, mold, Severe Acute Respiratory Syndrome (SARS), plague, smallpox, and needle stick hazards of human immunodeficiency virus (HIV), hepatitis B virus (HBV), and hepatitis C virus (HCV).

The ASP will reduce or eliminate the hazards of occupational exposure to blood borne pathogens, by implementing an exposure control plan for the worksite with details on employee protection measures. Engineering controls are the primary means of eliminating or minimizing employee exposure and include the use of safe devices in the work place, such as shielded needle devices, guards, or personal protective equipment (PPE) applications. The plan must also describe how an employer will use a combination of engineering and work practice controls, which include the use of personal protective clothing and equipment, training and documentation, medical surveillance, vaccinations, and signs and labels. Biological terrorism is an increasing concern for both emergency management and safety professionals to work together to design protection factors and mitigation methods.

Topic 2 - Chemical Hazards

What you need to know: Chemical hazards are common in the workplace. Workers must be protected from chemical hazards in any form (solid, liquid or gas). Examples are gases like acetylene, propane, carbon monoxide and helium, flammable materials like gasoline, solvents, and explosive chemicals, vapors and fumes that come from welding or exposure to solvents and liquids such as cleaning products, paints, acids, and solvents. Chemicals can cause illness, skin irritation, or breathing problems.

The Hazard Communication Standard states workers have the right to know and understand the hazardous chemicals they use and how to work with them safely and is covered under OSHA Hazard Communication - 1910.1200. In order to ensure chemical safety in the workplace, information about the identities and hazards of the chemicals must be available and understandable to workers. OSHA's Hazard Communication Standard (HCS) requires provision of information and training for manufacturers and importers to evaluate the hazards of the chemicals they produce or import, and prepare labels and safety data sheets to convey the hazard information to their downstream customers. All employers with hazardous chemicals in their workplaces must have labels and safety data sheets for their exposed workers, and train them to handle the chemicals appropriately.

New standards are in place as of 2013. The changes contained in the revised standard require the use of new labeling elements and a standardized format for Safety Data Sheets (SDSs), formerly known as, Material Safety Data Sheets (MSDSs). The standards are designed to improve worker understanding of the hazards associated with the chemicals in their workplace.

The 2013 **changes to the Hazard Communication Standard** include:

- **Hazard classification**: Provides specific criteria for classification of health and physical hazards, as well as classification of mixtures.
- **Labels**: Chemical manufacturers and importers will be required to provide a label that includes a harmonized signal word, pictogram, and hazard statement for each hazard class and category. Precautionary statements must also be provided.
- **Safety Data Sheets:** Will now have a specified 16-section format.
- **Information and training:** Employers are required to train workers on the new labels elements and safety data sheets format to facilitate recognition and understanding.

The ASP will provide training on the label elements which must include information on the type of information the employee would expect to see on the new labels including the **Product identifier:** how the hazardous chemical is identified. A **Signal word:** used to indicate the relative level of severity of hazard and alert the reader to a potential hazard on the label. There are only two signal words, "Danger" and "Warning." Within a specific hazard class, "Danger" is used for the more severe hazards and "Warning" is used for the less severe hazards. There will only be one signal word on the label no matter how many hazards a chemical may have. A **Pictogram with** OSHA's required pictogram in the shape of a square set at a point and include a black hazard symbol on a white background with a red frame sufficiently wide enough to be clearly visible. A square red frame set at a point without a hazard symbol is not a pictogram and is not permitted on the label. **Hazard**

statement(s) which describe the nature of the hazard(s) of a chemical, including the degree of hazard. **Precautionary statements** that describe recommended measures that should be taken to minimize or prevent adverse effects resulting from exposure to a hazardous chemical or improper storage or handling. Finally, the **Name, address and phone number of the chemical manufacturer, distributor, or importer** in the event of emergency.

Training on the format of the SDS must include information on the standardized 16-section format, including the type of information found in the various sections and how the information on the label is related to the SDS.

Topic 3 - Electrical Hazards

What you need to know: 29 CFR 1910 provides the basic guidance for OSHA's electrical standards. The standards are designed to protect employees exposed to dangers such as electric shock, electrocution, fires, and explosions. Electrical hazards are addressed in specific standards for the general industry, shipyard employment, and marine terminals.

Electrical hazards can cause burns, shocks and electrocution (death). General guidance provided to workers includes by OSHA include: Assume that all overhead wires are energized at lethal voltages. Never assume that a wire is safe to touch even if it is down or appears to be insulated. Never touch a fallen overhead power line. Call the electric utility company to report fallen electrical lines. Never operate electrical equipment while you are standing in water. Never repair electrical cords or equipment unless qualified and authorized. Always use caution when working near electricity.

When electrical shock enters the body it may produce both internal and external injury to body parts or the entire body and may result in death. After receiving a shock of electricity all or part of the body may be temporarily paralyzed which may cause loss of grip or stability. A person may also involuntarily move as a result of receiving an electrical shock, resulting in a fall. Factors which affect the severity of the shock include the voltage of the current, the presence of moisture, and the general health of the person prior to the shock. Low voltages can be extremely dangerous because the degree of injury increases the longer the body is in contact with the circuit.

The factors which affect the resistance of the body varies based on the amount of moisture on the skin (less moisture = more resistance), the size of the area of contact (smaller area = more resistance), the pressure applied to the contact point (less pressure = more resistance) and muscular structure (less muscle = less resistance).

Employees must not work near any part of an electric power circuit that the employee could contact in the course of work, unless the employee is protected against electric shock by de-energizing the circuit and grounding it or by guarding it effectively by insulation or other means.

Special Training is required for work on electrical equipment and only Authorized Employees may conduct electrical work. The training is must include:

- **Safe Work Practices**
- **Isolation of Electrical Sources**
- **Test Equipment**
- **Tools & PPE**

The ASP will recommend personal protective equipment, design appropriate engineering controls, be responsible to know the effects of electricity, and proper management for the OSHA standard for The Control of Hazardous Energy (Lockout/Tagout), Title 29 Code of Federal Regulations (CFR) Part 1910.147.

In general control circuit devices include push buttons, selector switches, and interlocks but may not be used as the sole means for de-energizing circuits or equipment. It is important to know the effects of the amount of AC Current where 1 ma=1/1000th of an amp. Common effects include:

- 3 ma - causes painful shock which cause indirect accidents
- 10ma - causes muscle contraction..."no let go" danger
- 30ma - possible lung paralysis- usually temporary

- 50ma - possible ventricular fibrillation (heart dysfunction, usually fatal)
- 100 ma - certain ventricular fibrillation resulting in fatality
- 4 amps - heart paralysis and severe burns

The OSHA standard for The Control of Hazardous Energy (Lockout/Tagout), Title 29 Code of Federal Regulations (CFR) Part 1910.147, addresses the practices and procedures necessary to disable machinery or equipment preventing the release of hazardous energy while employees perform servicing and maintenance activities.

Lock out tagout includes measures for controlling hazardous energies—electrical, mechanical,
hydraulic, pneumatic, chemical, thermal, and other energy sources. 29 CFR 1910.333 sets forth requirements to protect employees working on electric circuits and equipment. This includes requiring workers to use safe work practices including lockout and tagging procedures. These provisions apply when employees are exposed to electrical hazards while working on, near, or with conductors or systems that use electric energy.

According to OSAH compliance with the lockout/ tagout standard prevents an estimated 120 fatalities and 50,000 injuries each year. Workers injured on the job from exposure to hazardous
energy lose an average of 24 workdays for recuperation.

The ASP will be responsible to:

- Develop, document, implement, and enforce energy control procedures.
- Use lockout/tagout devices authorized for specific equipment or machinery and ensure that they are durable, standardized, and substantial.
- Ensure that lockout/tagout devices identify the individual users.
- Establish policy that permits only the employee who applied a lockout/tagout
- device to remove it.

- Inspect energy control procedures at least annually.
- Provide effective training for all employees covered by the standard.

- Comply with the additional energy control provisions in OSHA standards when machines or equipment must be tested or repositioned, when outside contractors work at the site, in group lockout situations, and during shift or personnel changes.

Topic 4 - Natural Hazards

What you need to know: Buildings, work environments and workers in any geographic location are subject to a wide variety of natural phenomena such as windstorms, floods, earthquakes, and other hazards. These occurrences cannot be predicted but their impacts are understood and can be managed effectively through a comprehensive program of hazard mitigation planning. Mitigation measures must be identified, prioritized, and implemented.

Natural hazards include earthquakes, hurricanes, typhoons, tornadoes, flooding, landslides and Mudslides, wild fire and tsunami.

The ASP will develop a hazard vulnerability analysis. Based on the hazard vulnerability analysis they will develop "shelter in place" measures, areas of refuge to protect facility occupants during an emergency, when evacuation may not be safe or possible due to area contamination, obstruction, or other hazard.

They will perform a risk assessment to identify likely threats and validate the need and design criteria for an area of refuge. Factors to be considered in the risk assessment process could include the type of hazard event, probability of event occurrence, severity of the event, probable consequences of a hazard, and a benefits/cost analysis of options.

They will coordinate planning, rehearsal, and preparatory procedures (routine maintenance/testing of equipment, checking shelf life of stored provisions and materials). Develop written standing operating procedures (SOP) outlining who makes decisions, when and how to evacuate, responsibilities and operating procedures, and when and how to leave the area of refuge. Planning may include, but is not limited to, personnel accountability protocol, communications for notification and instructions, comfort provisions, life-support systems such as fire apparatus, dedicated ventilation/filtration, plumbing, emergency power and storage for provisions of food, water, and first-aid.

Topic 5 - Radiation Hazards Knowledge Areas

1. Ionizing radiation

What you need to know: Ionizing radiation sources may be found in a wide range of occupational settings, including health care facilities, research institutions, nuclear weapon production facilities, and other various manufacturing settings. Radiation sources can pose a considerable health risk to affected workers if not properly controlled. Ionizing radiation is addressed in specific standards for the general industry, shipyard employment, and the construction industry.

Radioactive materials that decay produce ionizing radiation which has sufficient energy to strip away electrons from atoms (creating two charged ions) or to break some chemical bonds. Living tissue in the human body can be damaged by ionizing radiation as the body attempts to repair the damage, but sometimes the damage is of a nature that cannot be repaired or it is too severe or widespread to be repaired.

The amount and duration of radiation exposure affects the severity or type of health effect. There are two broad categories of health effects: stochastic and non-stochastic. Stochastic health effects are associated with long-term, low-level (chronic) exposure to radiation. Increased levels of exposure make these health effects more likely to occur, but do not influence the type or severity of the effect. Cancer is considered by most people the primary health effect from radiation exposure. Radiation can cause changes in DNA called mutations. Sometimes the body fails to repair these mutations or even creates mutations during repair. The mutations can be teratogenic or genetic. Teratogenic mutations are caused by exposure of the fetus in the uterus and affect only the individual who was exposed. Genetic mutations are passed on to offspring. Non-stochastic effects appear in cases of exposure to high levels of radiation, and become more severe as the exposure increases. Short-term, high-level exposure is referred to as 'acute' exposure. Many non-cancerous health effects of radiation are non-stochastic. Unlike cancer, health effects from 'acute' exposure to radiation usually appear quickly. Acute health effects include burns and radiation sickness. Radiation sickness is also called 'radiation poisoning.' It can cause premature aging or even death. If the dose is fatal, death usually occurs within two months. The symptoms of radiation sickness include: nausea, weakness, hair loss, skin burns or diminished organ function.

2. Nonionizing radiation is a series of energy waves composed of oscillating electric and magnetic fields traveling at the speed of light.

Non-ionizing radiation includes the spectrum of ultraviolet (UV), visible light, infrared (IR), microwave (MW), radio frequency (RF), and extremely low frequency (ELF). Extremely Low Frequency (ELF) radiation at 60 HZ are those produced by power lines, electrical wiring, and electrical equipment. Microwave radiation (MW) is absorbed near the skin, while Radiofrequency (RF) radiation may be absorbed throughout the body. Infrared Radiation (IR) would include types of radiation the skin and eyes absorb as heat. Workers normally notice excessive exposure through heat sensation and pain. Visible Light Radiation includes the different visible frequencies of the electromagnetic (EM) spectrum seen by eyes as different colors. Ultraviolet radiation (UV) has a high photon energy range and is particularly hazardous because there are usually no immediate symptoms of excessive exposure. Sources of UV radiation include the sun, black lights, welding arcs, and UV lasers. Lasers typically emit optical (UV, visible light, IR) radiations and are primarily an eye and skin hazard. Common lasers include CO_2 IR laser, helium - neon, neodymium YAG and the Nitrogen UV laser.

The ASP will be responsible for exposure controls and training in both forms of radiation.

Topic 6 Structural and Mechanical Hazards

Structural collapse is second only to falls as a cause of fatalities. Stability is essential to the successful erection of any structure. Structural stability is provided through use of shear connectors (such as headed steel studs, steel bars, or steel lugs), reinforcing bars, and anchors. Structural hazards may also in include tripping hazards and the need to cover roof and floor openings. Covers for roof and floor openings shall be capable of supporting, without failure, twice the weight of the employees, equipment, and materials that may be imposed on them at any one time.

Mechanical hazards are created by the powered operation of apparatus or tools. The applied power may be electrical or human. Tools or apparatus have three locations where mechanical hazards can exist: the point of operation, the point of power transmission, and the area of moving parts.

The ASP will be responsible for inspection of structural and mechanical hazards and training required for minimizing risks related to these hazards. Identifying hazards is the first step toward protecting workers. The basic types of hazardous mechanical motions and actions are cutting, punching, shearing, and bending

Safeguards must meet these minimum general requirements:

- Prevent contact where the safeguard must prevent hands, arms or any other part of a worker's body from making contact with dangerous moving parts.
- Allow safe lubrication and if possible, one should be able to lubricate the machine without removing the safeguard.
- Be secure so workers should not be able to easily remove or tamper with the safeguard. They must be firmly secure to the machine where possible or secured elsewhere if attachment to the machine is not possible.
- The safeguard should protect from falling objects so that no objects can fall into moving parts.
- A safeguard should create no new hazards and defeats its purpose if it creates a hazard such as a shear point, a jagged edge or an unfinished surface.
- A safeguard should create no interference because any safeguard that impedes a worker from performing a job quickly and comfortably might soon be bypassed or disregarded. Proper safeguarding can actually enhance efficiency because it relieves a worker's injury apprehensions.

Topic 7 Hazards Related to Fires and Explosions

Both the Occupational Safety and Health Administration (OSHA) and the National Fire Protection Association (NFPA) have written standards and regulations that build on one another and help keep all workers safer from hazards in the workplace.

The ASP should be knowledgeable of explosive atmospheres which can be caused by flammable gases, mists, vapors or combustible dusts. Industrial atmospheres and confined spaces both present risk if there is enough of a flammable substance mixed with air and an available source of ignition.

Liquids such as petroleum based products, fuels and solvents give off flammable vapor which, when mixed with air, can ignite or explode. The ease by which liquids give off flammable vapors is linked to a simple physical test called Flashpoint in which the minimum temperature at which a liquid, under specific test conditions, gives off sufficient flammable vapor to ignite momentarily on the application of an ignition source.

Extremely flammable liquids have a flashpoint lower than 0°C and a boiling point lower than or equal to 35°C. **Highly flammable** liquids have a flashpoint below 21°C but which are not extremely flammable. **Flammable** liquids have a flashpoint equal to or greater than 21°C and less than or equal to 55°C support combustion when tested in the prescribed manner at 55°C.

Dusts can form explosive atmospheres and are classed as dangerous substances. A cloud of combustible dust in the air can explode violently if there is a source of ignition. **Solids** include materials such as plastic foam, packaging, and textiles which can burn fiercely and give off dense black smoke, sometimes poisonous.

Topic 8 Hazards Related to Human Factors and Ergonomics

1. Fitness for duty

Pre-employment screening has two major functions the ASP must know: 1) determination of an individual's fitness for duty, including the ability to work while wearing protective equipment, and 2) provision of baseline data for comparison with future medical data. Workers can be required to perform strenuous tasks and wear personal protective equipment, such as respirators and protective clothing, that may cause heat stress and other problems .To ensure that prospective employees are able to meet work requirements a pre-employment screening should focus on the following areas:

Perform an occupational and medical history paying special attention to prior occupational exposures to chemical and physical hazards.

- Review past illnesses and chronic diseases such as asthma, lung diseases, and cardiovascular disease.
- Review symptoms such as shortness of breath or labored breathing on exertion, other chronic respiratory symptoms, chest pain, high blood pressure, and heat intolerance.
- Record relevant lifestyle habits such as cigarette smoking, alcohol and drug use, and off duty hobbies.
- Perform a comprehensive physical examination of all body organs, focusing on the pulmonary, cardiovascular, and musculoskeletal systems.
- Note conditions that could affect PPE usage and disqualify individuals who are clearly unable to perform based on the medical history and physical examination.
- Pre-employment screening can be used to establish baseline data to subsequently verify the efficacy of protective assures and to later determine if exposures have adversely affected the worker. Baseline testing may include both medical screening tests and biologic monitoring tests. The latter (e.g., blood lead level) may be useful for ascertaining pre-exposure levels of specific substances to which the worker may be exposed and for which reliable tests are available.

2. Manual materials handling

You need to know available equipment and engineering controls to assist in material handling. Material handling involves diverse operations such as hoisting, carrying bags or materials manually, stacking palletized bricks or other materials such as drums, barrels, kegs, and lumber. In addition to training and education, workers should understand the potential hazards and be able to recognize the methods for eliminating or minimizing the occurrence of such accidents. Back injuries are most common relating to bending, followed by twisting and turning. Other hazards include falling objects, improperly stacked materials, and strains and sprains from lifting loads improperly or from carrying loads that are either too large or too heavy, as well as fractures and bruises caused by being struck by materials or by being caught in pinch points.

When moving materials manually employees must always wear appropriate personal protective equipment, use proper lifting techniques, and use assistance if needed human or lifting assist device.

3. Organizational, behavioral, and psychological influences

Workers who are concerned for their safety or physical or psychological health in a work environment in which their safety and health is not perceived as a priority, will not be able to provide error-free work. Working safely depends on an employee or workers current needs, present situation, psyche, and past experiences. The lack of a safety culture as a contributing factor to noncompliance with safety and hazard control.

To effectively impact the organizational and behavioral influences the ASP will ensure management takes action, workers participate in safety planning, appropriate PPE is available, influence is instituted in the group norms regarding acceptable safety practices, hazard identification and assessment occurs, hazard prevention and control, education and training, and program evaluation and improvement are continually refined. Prevention, encouragement and enforcement are key.

4. Physical and mental stressors

Studies have provided ample evidence of the effect of psycho-social factors at work on health and well-being. Stressors include monotonous work, tight deadlines, bullying, job insecurity and long-working hours, which constitute collective elements. There is a clear parallel between the scientific literature regarding the design of work as a means of increasing motivation and organizational effectiveness and work design as a means for improving individual well-being.

Stress management is the physiological response to a psychological event or a change.
- The effects of adaptation on the body are referred to as a stress response.
- Stress is the body's response to anything the mind perceives or imagines to be threatening, frustrating, or demanding. It has both physical and emotional components.
- Shift work, sleep deprivation, overtime, inadequate resources, unfamiliarity with a job lack of supervision and exposure to biological or chemical hazards may lead to stress. The ASP will assist in planning and engineering controls to reduce the risk by providing open communication, a stress management program, flexibility within departments, work rotation and equipment recommendations.

5. Repetitive activities

Ergonomic injuries and occupational repetitive stress injuries (RSIs) comprise more than one hundred different types of job-induced injuries and illnesses resulting from wear and tear on the body. RSIs are one of the fastest growing workplace injuries, and can result any time there is a mismatch between the physical requirements of the job and the physical capacity of the human body. Specific risk factors that can cause RSIs include repetitive motion, force, awkward posture, heavy lifting, or a combination of these factors.

The ASP is responsible for knowledge of the causes and application of standards for the ergonomic program. This includes improving system designs to eliminate a problem, precluding worker development of cumulative trauma disorders, focus on structural response and human adaptation to stress through biomechanical analysis.
- Cumulative trauma disorders are illnesses that develop over time, ANSI has standards for CTD's and the World Health Organization provides ergonomic definitions.

- Ergonomic assessments include evaluation of same motion pattern, awkward posture for two hours, vibration or impact over two hours, manual lifting more than twice a work shift, workstation or work shift work that is electronically or mechanically paced for more than four hours.
- Medical management provides identification, evaluation, and treatment.
- ASP's provide education, workstation evaluation, and evaluation and analysis of problems or complaints such as absenteeism and turnover rates.

6. Workplace violence

Workplace violence is violence or the threat of violence against workers. It can occur at or
outside the workplace and can range from threats and verbal abuse to physical assaults and
homicide as one of the leading causes of job-related deaths. OSHA's General Duty Clause requires employers to provide a safe and healthful workplace for all workers.

Workplace violence programs have five core elements:
- Written procedures - zero tolerance and communication
- Worksite analysis - establishment of a threat assessment
- Prevention and control measures – engineering and security controls
- Training and education – potential risks, diffusion, and protection
- Recordkeeping and program evaluation – OSHA logs and medical reports

Safety Fundamentals Examination Domain 2

Measuring, Evaluating, and Controlling Safety, Health, and Environmental Hazards 30.9%

Topic 1 - Measurement and Monitoring
Knowledge Areas

1. Methods and techniques for measurement, sampling, and analysis

Chemical sampling and analysis is used by occupational health and safety professionals to assess workplace contaminants and associated worker exposures. The validity of an assessment is based on the procedures used for sample collection and analysis, and data interpretation. The ASP will understand the multitude of variables within a specific workplace that require the safety professional to exercise judgment in the design of a particular assessment. When workers are exposed to chemicals, it's important to make sure they are not overexposed. Chemical monitoring can be monitored in several ways. To sample worker exposure, diffusion-detector tubes, vapor-monitoring badges, or personal air-sampling pumps can be used. To monitor specific work areas, detector tubes and pumps, hand-held electronic monitors, or fixed wall-mounted electronic monitors are used.

The ASP needs to know these basic definitions related to air sampling and analysis:

Ceiling is the concentration of chemical exposure that must not be exceeded during any part of the workday.

General-area sampling is used to determine whether an area is hazardous or becomes hazardous while the workers are present.

Immediately dangerous to life or health (IDLH) are conditions that pose an immediate threat to life or health, or conditions that pose an immediate threat of severe exposure to contaminants.

Lower-explosive level (LEL) are the lower limits of flammability of a gas or vapor at ordinary ambient temperature expressed in percentage of the gas or vapor in air volume. The limit is assumed constant for temperatures up to 120°C (250°F). Above this temperature you should decrease it by a factor of 0.7 because explosive tendencies increase with higher temperatures.

Milligrams per cubic meter (mg/m3) is the unit used to measure air concentration of dust, gases, mists and fumes.

Parts per million (PPM) is the measure for parts of air by volume of vapor, gas or other contaminant.

Permissible exposure limits (PELs) are the Occupational Safety and Health's time-weighted average concentration that must not be exceeded during any eight-hour work shift of a 40-hour workweek. **PELs** are found in 29 CFR 1910.1000 in the Z-1A or Z-2 tables.

Personal sampling is sampling done to evaluate a worker's exposure during the workday typically worn in the breathing zone.

Short-term exposure limits (STEL) are concentrations measured over a 15-minute period unless otherwise noted.

Time-weighted average (TWA) is the concentrations of airborne toxic materials that have been weighted for a certain time, usually eight hours.

Threshold-limit value (TLV) is an eight-hour time-weighted average concentration set up by the American Conference of Governmental Industrial Hygienists (ACGIH). They are used as a recommended level.

Upper-explosive level (UEL) is the highest concentration, expressed in percentage of vapor or gas in the air by volume of a substance that will burn or explode when an ignition source is present.

- Use diffusion detector tubes, personal badges or personal air-sampling pumps to measure a worker's exposure to hazardous chemicals.
- Use detector tubes or a hand held monitor to measure the current level of hazard or how hazardous an area is.

- Consult your owner's manual for recommended calibration timeframes. Monitors should be calibrated daily or before every use to ensure that your workers are safe.
- When working with confined spaces know what types of hazards to expect. Then monitor for oxygen, then combustible gas, and then any toxic gases that might be present. This is typically done with a three or four-gas monitor.
- For a tube which reads in percent volume 1% = 10,000 ppm
- PPM = (mg/m3 x 24.45) / molecular weight

2. Uses and limitations of monitoring equipment

Diffusion-Detector Tubes

Several manufacturers make diffusion-detector tubes, which have limited applications. Diffusion tubes can be used to determine a time-weighted average (TWA) or a short-term exposure limit (STEL). They usually consist of a glass tube with a chemical reagent impregnated in a silica layer. One end is broken off and the tube is placed in a tube holder. If the tube has a clip, it is often hung on the worker's lapel, near the breathing zone, to get an accurate reading of the worker's exposure. To calculate an accurate level, the sampling start time must be recorded on the writing area of the tube. Diffusion-detector tubes meet are not the most accurate method of air sampling.

Advantages: They give an immediate reading, and you don't have to wait for lab results.
Limitations: There are often cross chemical sensitivities.

Vapor-Monitor Badges

Vapor-monitor badges are a good way to monitor a worker's breathing zone to determine the worker's exposure. Badges are worn on the collar. The exposure time, temperature, relative humidity, date exposed, employee and monitor number must be recorded to calculate the exposure level. The badges can be used to determine an eight-hour time-weighted average or a 15-minute short-term exposure limit. Badges are available for organic vapors, formaldehyde, ethylene oxide, mercury, nitrous oxide and other compounds.

Advantages: The results are more accurate than those of diffusion tubes.
Limitations: Badges have to be sent away to a laboratory for analysis and results cannot be given immediately and badges are also only available for a limited number of chemicals.

Personal Air-Sampling Pumps

Personal air-sampling pumps consist of a small pump that pulls a constant amount of air (usually in liters per minute), a charcoal tube or filter cassette, and a clip for attaching the collection media near the worker's breathing zone.

These pumps require calibration before each use and must have the flow rate set to the correct level depending on what is being monitored. The worker usually wears the pump and the collection media for the entire day. Once the day is finished, the charcoal tube or filter cassette is sent to the laboratory of choice to be analyzed.

Advantages: The results are usually more accurate than other methods and allow for a broader sampling of chemicals. It is also one of the few ways to get a time-weighted average for dusts in the air.
Limitations: Requires a knowledge of National Institute for Occupational Safety and Health (NIOSH) sampling methods.

Detector Tubes and Pumps

Detector tube and pump systems effective for on-the-spot air monitoring. They are accurate enough to get an idea of the hazards in the workplace and are typically used when surveying an area to get an idea of worker exposure in ppm or percent volume. Two main types of pumps are available: piston and bellows. The piston style requires the user to pull a piston to pull air through the tube. With the bellows style, the user squeezes the bellow, and upon release, air is pulled through the tube as the bellow opens.

Tubes are available in, scale tube, qualitative tube, pretube, color matching tube, and color comparison tube.

Advantages: Allow for quick sampling of an area and are relatively inexpensive for quick monitoring.
Limitations: The tubes are limited in the types of chemicals they can pick up and certain chemicals can interfere with the tubes and give false readings.

Hand-Held Electronic Monitors

Continuous hand-held monitors can vary from a relatively simple single-gas monitor to complex four-gas monitors. They make a quantitative analysis that is displayed on a digital or analog readout.
Advantages: The results are immediate and most hand-held meters also have a visible or audible alarm or both that will alert the user if a gas is above a safe level.
Limitations: Hand held meters are usually calibrated with one type of gas, and interference from similar gases could alter the readings. The operator must have adequate training to interpret the information that the monitor is providing and be familiar with calibration and limitations of the device.

Fixed-Air Monitors

Fixed monitors use sensors that have a wide range of chemicals that they can monitor. They are in a fixed location and operate at all times. They often have alarms to alert workers to a dangerous situation.

Make sure you understand what the monitor will and will not do.

Topic 2 - Engineering Controls

The concept behind engineering controls is that the work environment and the job being performed should be designed to eliminate hazards or reduce exposure to hazards. Engineering controls have the potential to completely eliminate a hazard, and do not rely on human behavior to be effective. A common example is a ventilation system which requires no management in comparison to respiratory protection which must be monitored, inspected, trained, and managed.

Implementing engineering controls reduces the potential for exposure and involves developing work practices to prevent workplace hazards.

Some ways to prevent and control hazards are:
- Ensure that hazard correction procedures are in place.
- If feasible, design the facility, equipment, or process to remove the hazard or substitute something that is not hazardous.
- Make sure that employees understand and follow safe work procedures.
- Ensure there is a medical program tailored to your facility to help prevent workplace hazards and exposures.
- Ensure that employees know how to use and maintain personal protective equipment.
- Regularly and thoroughly maintain equipment.

- If removal is not feasible, enclose the hazard to prevent exposure in normal operations.

The systems used to prevent and control hazards include Engineering Controls, Safe Work Practices, and Administrative Controls. Prevention methods include Personal Protective Equipment (PPE), Systems to Track Hazard Correction, Preventive Maintenance Systems, Emergency Preparation, and Medical Programs.

1. Dust control

Dust control may be required in processing, handling or generating particulate matter. Dust control practices may be required in any of the following applications, fertilizer production, woodworking, painting, powdered foodstuff, spice mixing and packaging, ceramic cutting, grinding, powdered chemical processing and packaging are just a few of the applications for which it is critical.

The methods used to keep particulate from one space from contaminating another include:
- Barrier separation which is a wall or partition between affected areas.
- Local exhaust which is a high velocity airflow stream captures particles at the point they are generated and carries them away.
- Exhaust with filtration which is a high velocity airflow stream captures particles and recirculates them through a filter medium where they are removed.
- Area exhaust which is a high volume exhaust fan draws air from the full room volume to an outside vent or recirculates through a filtration or separation device.

2. Equipment and material handling

Material Handling Equipment may include a range of tools, vehicles, appliances and accessories involved in transporting, storing, controlling, and protecting products at any stage of manufacturing, distribution, consumption, or disposal. The four main categories of material handling equipment include storage, engineered systems, industrial trucks and bulk material handling.

Storage and Handling Equipment includes non-automated materials such as storage equipment used to hold or buffer materials during downtime or times when they are not being transported. Examples are shelves, bins and drawers, pallet racks, drive-through or drive-in racks, push-back racks, sliding racks, and stacking frames.

Engineered systems work cohesively to enable storage and transportation. An example of an engineered system is an Automated Storage and Retrieval System which is a large automated organizational structure involving racks, aisles and shelves accessible by mechanized cherry picker that can be used by a worker or can perform fully automated functions reducing risk of injury.

Industrial Trucks refer to transportation items and vehicles used to move materials and products in materials handling. These transportation devices can include small hand-operated trucks, pallet-jacks, order pickers, side loaders and various kinds of forklifts.

Bulk material handling refers to the storing, transportation and control of materials in loose bulk form. These include food, liquid, grain or materials moved by conveyor belts or elevators designed to move large quantities of material, or in packaged form, through the use of drums and hoppers. These include conveyor belts, grain elevators, reclaimers, and hoppers.

3. Excavation shoring

You need to know excavating is recognized as one of the most hazardous construction operations. OSHA standards include 29 CFR 1926.650, 29 CFR 1926.651, and 29 CFR 1926.652. The ASP should permit the use of performance criteria where possible, and provide construction employers with options when classifying soil and selecting employee protection methods.

Dangers of Trenching and Excavation include cave-ins pose the greatest risk and are much more likely than other excavation-related accidents to result in worker fatalities. Other potential hazards for excavation include falls, falling loads, hazardous atmospheres, and incidents involving mobile equipment.

Trench Safety Measures include trenches 5 feet (1.5 meters) deep or greater require a protective system unless the excavation is made entirely in stable rock. If less than 5 feet deep, a competent person may determine that a protective system is not required. Trenches 20 feet (6.1 meters) deep or greater require that the protective system be designed by a registered professional engineer.

For trenching purposes OSHA defines a **competent person** as one who inspects trenches daily and as conditions change by a before worker entry to ensure elimination of excavation hazards. A competent person is an individual who is capable of identifying existing and predictable hazards or working conditions that are hazardous, unsanitary, or dangerous to workers, soil types and protective systems required, and who is authorized to take prompt corrective measures to eliminate these hazards and conditions.

4. Facility physical security

Facility physical requirements are the facility and building security safeguards designed to prevent incidents. The ASP will check geographical factors, configuration of space, entrances, fire safety and fire protection, utilities, electrical closets and conduit runs, heating and cooling systems, water supplies, and boilers and generators, sensitive activities, and contingency plans.

5. Fall protection

OSHA has adopted several regulations pertaining to construction fall protection currently subpart E, personal protective equipment and in subpart M fall protection. These systems and standards are intended to prevent employees from falling off, onto or through working levels and to protect employees from falling objects. Any fall rescue program should take as little time as possible to bring a fallen worker to safety. Any rescue plan should be regularly reviewed to ensure that the procedures are manageable and realistic in their time estimates.

Know the definition and application of competent person. Training requirements include providing a training program for each employee who might be exposed to fall hazards. The program shall enable each employee to recognize the hazards of falling and shall train each employee in the procedures to be followed in order to minimize these hazards. The training is to be provided by a competent person qualified in the following areas:

- The nature of fall hazards in the work area.
- The role of employees in fall protection plans.
- The correct procedures for erecting, maintaining, disassembling, and inspecting the fall protection systems to be used.
- The use and operation of guardrail systems, personal fall arrest systems, safety net systems, warning line systems, safety monitoring systems, controlled access zones and other protection to be used.
- The role of each employee in the safety monitoring system when this system is used.
- The limitations on the use of mechanical equipment during the performance of roofing work on low-sloped roofs.
- The correct procedures for the handling and storage of equipment and materials and the erection of overhead protection.

6. Fire prevention, protection, and suppression

Fire prevention, protection, and suppression measures are used to protect employees and facilities from the dangers of fire to reduce the risk of potential injuries, death and property damage. Fire suppression systems are to be inspected regularly and maintained employees are to be trained to use evacuation routes and procedures. The ASP will train and review procedures for monitoring the use of flammable materials and ensuring that storage areas for flammables are maintained properly.

Fires are classified according to the type of fuel or material:
- Class A—wood, paper and cloth
- Class B—flammable gases, liquids and greases
- Class C—fires in live electrical equipment, or involving materials near electrically powered equipment
- Class D—combustible metals such as magnesium, zirconium, potassium and sodium

Key points:
- Review sources of open flame such as welding and cutting torches, furnaces, matches and heaters.
- Prohibit cutting or welding equipment containing flammable liquids unless the equipment has been emptied and purged with a neutral gas such as nitrogen.
- Eliminate the possibility of static sparks in flammable storage or handling areas.
- Prohibit chemical ignition sources i.e. DC motors, switches and circuit breakers) in areas where flammable materials are stored or handled.
- Use only non-sparking tools in areas where flammables are stored or handled.
- Store materials such as oxidizers and organic peroxides, which produce large amounts of oxygen when they decompose, in an area separate from flammable materials.

Fire extinguishers should be maintained using NFPA standards. Site inspections should ensure compliance with the Fire Safety Program. These inspections should address housekeeping issues, proper storage of chemicals, access to fire extinguishers and emergency evacuation routes. Every exit must be clearly visible, or the path to it conspicuously identified in such a manner that every occupant of the building will know the best way to get out of the building in a fire or other emergency. Exits must never be obstructed.

7. Hazardous energy control

Hazardous energy control includes energy sources including electrical, mechanical, hydraulic, pneumatic, chemical, thermal or other sources in machines and equipment can be hazardous to workers. During the servicing and maintenance of machines and equipment, the unexpected startup or release of stored energy could cause injury to employees.

Injuries from hazardous energy control may include electrocution, burns, crushing, cutting, lacerating, amputating, or fracturing body parts, and others.

Proper lockout/tagout (LOTO) practices and procedures safeguard workers from the release of hazardous energy. OSHA's Lockout tagout describes the practices and procedures necessary to disable machinery or equipment to prevent the release of hazardous energy. The OSHA standard for The Control of Hazardous Energy is 29 CFR 1910.147 for general industry and outlines measures for controlling different types of hazardous energy. The LOTO standard establishes the employer's responsibility to protect workers from hazardous energy.

Lock out tagout training requires employees who work in the area where the energy control procedures are utilized need to be instructed in the purpose and use of the energy control procedures and about the prohibition against attempting to restart or reenergize machines or equipment that is locked or tagged out.

All employees who are authorized to lockout machines or equipment and perform the service and maintenance operations need to be trained in recognition of applicable hazardous energy sources in the workplace and the means and methods of isolating or controlling the energy.

Retraining is required for all employees to maintain proficiency or introduce new or changed control methods.

8. Human factors and ergonomic design

Human factors engineering and ergonomic design requires an interdisciplinary approach to evaluating and improving the safety, efficiency, and robustness of work systems. Human factors engineering includes the intersection of people, technology, policy, and work across multiple domains, using an interdisciplinary approach including

- **Task Analysis and Design** - such as observations of work in situ, structured interviews of employees, and simulation studies. Task analysis data shows the cognitive demands of work and employees adapt to it.
- **Device Evaluation and Usability** – Includes development of use of devices, IT systems, and other tools to support the human component of modern work systems.
- **Communication, Collaboration, and Teamwork** – helps evaluate ergonomic design across the organization to design better tools and techniques and incorporate training.

9. Mechanical and machine guarding

Machine Guarding involves protection for moving machine parts have the potential to cause severe workplace injuries, such as crushed fingers or hands, amputations, burns, or blindness. Any machine part, function, or process that may cause injury must be safeguarded. When the operation of a machine or accidental contact injure the operator or others in the vicinity, the hazards must be eliminated or controlled. Machines need to be guarded according to the requirements of the Code of Federal Regulations (CFR) 29 CFR 1910 Subpart O: Machinery and Machine Guarding (29 CFR 1910.211-219).

Machine guarding key requirements include:

- Guards need to be durable and require tools to remove them so that the machine operator cannot alter, modify, or move.
- If a machine is located where no employees have access to it (guarded by location), no additional guarding is required.
- If repairs need to be done on machinery, and this exposes employees to moving parts, an alternative way to prevent such exposure is to lock out the piece of equipment according to the requirements of 29 CFR 1910.147.
- Employees need to be trained on how to use some adjustable guards and in all cases trained not to remove guards because they may seem to be in the way.

10. Segregation and separation

Engineering controls for the separation and segregation of hazards. **Separation** includes isolation of the hazard, placing distance between the hazard and employee, and implementing system design and remodel which protect the employee. **Segregation** is used when separation is not possible it isolates a hazard by using a barrier to implement a control without burdening an entire facility resulting in non-adherence to safety guidelines. Housekeeping, ventilation, hazard assessment, and explosion prevention and mitigation are all activities under segregation and separation.

11. Substitution and selection of alternative design strategies

Substitution and selection of alternative design strategies involves determination of requirements, requirements restructuring, alternative generation and selection of safety activities, processes, or PPE. Alternative safety processes or activities are then based on new functional requirements, evaluation of the environmental application and subsequent implementation.

12. Ventilation

You need to know OSHA standards cover ventilation requirements for a variety of operations including abrasive blasting, grinding or polishing, and spay finishing operations. Remember OSHA's permissible exposure limit for carbon monoxide is 5000 ppm.

Mechanical ventilation engineering standards are guided by these standards:
- ASHRAE standard Ventilation for Acceptable Indoor Air Quality
- NFPA 90A Standard for the Installation of Air Conditioning and Ventilation Systems.
- ANSI Z9.2-160 Design and Operation of Local Exhaust Systems
- 29 CFR 1910 air contaminants

Engineering controls are local and mechanical to include fume hoods and ventilation.

Topic 3 - Administrative Controls

Administrative controls (or work practice controls) are changes in work procedures such as written safety policies, rules, supervision, schedules, and training with the goal of reducing the duration, frequency, and severity of exposure to hazardous chemicals or situations.

As with work practice controls, administrative controls normally are used in conjunction with other controls that more directly prevent or control exposure to hazard.

1. Accountability

You need to know employees should be responsible for their own safety activity. It is the employers' responsibility to ensure safety rules and regulations are followed. Accountability as an administrative control includes safety training and documentation, retraining, and documentation of noncompliance.

2. Behavior modification

You need to know behavior based safety is a method to use positive reinforcement to change unsafe behaviors. It focuses on preventing unsafe behavior, encouraging safe behavior, and establishing and enforcing safety rules.

3. Decontamination processes

Process safety management for decontamination is the combination of physical and chemical processes that kills or removes biological, chemical, radiological or other contaminate exposures.

The decontamination process includes the usage of disinfectants and other chemicals to reduce human contact and exposure of soaps and detergents, oxidizing agents, alkalis, acids, aldehydes, insecticides. Proper donn and doff of PPE and and engineering controls to minimize PEL and STEL exposure limits is required.

4. Exposure limitation

The **permissible exposure limit (PEL) is** the legal in the United States for exposure of an employee to a chemical substance or physical agent. Chemical exposure is expressed in parts per million (ppm) or in milligrams per cubic meter (mg/m^3). Permissible exposure limits are established by the Occupational Safety and Health Administration (OSHA). A PEL is usually given as a **time-weighted average (TWA)** some are short-term exposure limits (STEL) or ceiling limits. A TWA is the average exposure over a specified period of time typically a nominal eight hours. For limited periods a worker may be exposed to concentrations higher than the PEL as the average concentration over eight hours remains lower. Units of measure for physical agents such as noise are specific to the agent. **A short-term exposure limit (STEL)** is one that addresses the average exposure over a 15-30 minute period of maximum exposure during a single work shift. **A ceiling limit is one that may not be exceeded for any period of time** and is applied to irritants and other materials that have immediate effects.

5. Fitness for duty

Fitness for duty as an administrative control requires an analysis of an employee's preexisting conditions and present health in relation to their job position and ability to perform tasks utilizing the appropriate PPE.

6. Housekeeping

Housekeeping administrative controls include training of employees to decontaminate work surfaces and equipment, properly store supplies and equipment, organize, arrange and perform work in a clean and efficient manner. Housekeeping should include checklists and periodic inspections.

7. Labels

The ASP will be required to know the common requirements for labeling of hazardous materials and for training employees on the Hazard Communication Standards. OSHA has updated the requirements for labeling of hazardous chemicals under the Hazard Communication Standard (HCS). By June 1, 2015, all labels will be required to have pictograms, a signal word, hazard and precautionary statements, the product identifier, and supplier identification. A sample revised HCS label identifying the required label elements is shown below.

SAMPLE LABEL

PRODUCT IDENTIFIER

CODE _____
Product Name _____

SUPPLIER IDENTIFICATION

Company Name _____
Street Address _____
City _____ State _____
Postal Code _____ Country _____
Emergency Phone Number _____

PRECAUTIONARY STATEMENTS

Keep container tightly closed. Store in cool, well ventilated place that is locked.
Keep away from heat/sparks/open flame. No smoking.
Only use non-sparking tools.
Use explosion-proof electrical equipment.
Take precautionary measure against static discharge.
Ground and bond container and receiving equipment.
Do not breathe vapors.
Wear Protective gloves.
Do not eat, drink or smoke when using this product.
Wash hands thoroughly after handling.
Dispose of in accordance with local, regional, national, international regulations as specified.

In Case of Fire: use dry chemical (BC) or Carbon dioxide (CO_2) fire extinguisher to extinguish.

First Aid

HAZARD PICTOGRAMS

SIGNAL WORD
Danger

HAZARD STATEMENT

**Highly flammable liquid and vapor.
May cause liver and kidney damage.**

SUPPLEMENTAL INFORMATION

Directions for use

_____
_____
_____

Fill weight: _____ Lot Number _____

Gross weight: _____ Fill Date: _____
Expiration Date: _____

www.OSHA.gov

8. Material safety data sheets

Material safety data sheets are now replaced with Hazard Communication Safety Data Sheets

The Hazard Communication Standard (HCS) requires chemical manufacturers, distributors, or importers to provide Safety Data Sheets (SDSs) (formerly known as Material Safety Data Sheets or MSDSs) to communicate the hazards of hazardous chemical products. The following are adapted from the Hazard Communication Standard.

Section 1. Identification includes product identifier; manufacturer or distributor name, address, phone number; emergency phone number; recommended use; restrictions on use.

Section 2. Hazard(s) identification includes all hazards regarding the chemical; required label elements.

Section 3. Composition/information on ingredients includes information on chemical ingredients; trade secret claims.

Section 4. First-aid measures includes important symptoms/ effects, acute, delayed; required treatment.

Section 5. Fire-fighting measures lists suitable extinguishing techniques, equipment; chemical hazards from fire.

Section 6. Accidental release measures lists emergency procedures; protective equipment; proper methods of containment and cleanup.

Section 7. Handling and storage lists precautions for safe handling and storage, including incompatibilities.

Section 8. Exposure controls/personal protection lists OSHA's Permissible Exposure Limits (PELs); Threshold Limit Values (TLVs); appropriate engineering controls; personal protective equipment (PPE).

Section 9. Physical and chemical properties lists the chemical's characteristics.

Section 10. Stability and reactivity lists chemical stability and possibility of hazardous reactions.

Section 11. Toxicological information includes routes of exposure; related symptoms, acute and chronic effects; numerical measures of toxicity.

Section 12, Ecological information, Section 13, Disposal considerations, Section 14, Transport information, Section 15, Regulatory information.

9. Safe work permits

A safe work permit is document that identifies the work to be done, the hazard(s) involved, and the precautions to be taken. It ensures that all hazards and precautions have been considered before work begins. The permit is authorizes specific work, at a specific work location, for a specific time period.

The safe work permit is an agreement between the issuer and the receiver that documents the conditions, preparations, precautions, and limitations of the work to be accomplished that need to be clearly understood before work begins. Permits are used for controlling and co-ordinating work to establish and maintain safe working conditions.

Work permits may be required by OSHA specifically for lockout/tagout standards, 29 CFR 1910.147, Hot Work Permits, Electrical work permits, and Confined Space Entry Permit.

General contents of a permit include

- Description of circuit/equipment/job location.
- Description of work to be done.
- Detailed job description procedure to be used in performing the above detailed work.

- Description of the safe work practices to be employed.
- Results of the hazard analysis
- Necessary personal protective equipment to safety perform the assigned task.
- Means employed to restrict the access of unqualified persons from the work area.
- Evidence of completion of job briefing including discussion of any job-related hazards.

10. Training and education

Training and education as an administrative control should include elements where **supervisors** can explain rules, procedures, and work practices for hazard control and how they teach and enforce them. **Employees** should understand safe work procedures and how to protect themselves and where PPE is required with its limitations and maintenance requirements.

11. Warnings and signs

Warnings and signs are explicit in their usage and application. Warning signs are to be clear and concise containing signaling words with emergency, warning and fire information.

The ASP needs to know color codes for safety are governed by 29 CFR 1910.144 and ANSI Z53.1. Accident prevention signs and tags are governed by 29 CFR 1910.145. Piping systems are governed by ANSI A13.1.

Red denotes danger, yellow denotes caution, blue indicates a warning, green is used for safety equipment, magenta and yellow are used for radiation, black and white are used for traffic boundaries, and orange is used to mark dangerous parts of equipment.

12. Work zone establishment

Work zone establishment as an administrative control requires the ASP to know how establish or perform analysis on site preparation, site work zones, exclusion zones, contamination reduction support zone, buddy systems, communication systems, and safe work practices.

Topic 4 - Personal Protective Equipment

Personal protective equipment, or PPE, is designed to protect workers from serious workplace injuries or illnesses resulting from contact with chemical, radiological, physical,
electrical, mechanical, or other workplace hazards.

In general these may include face shields, safety glasses, hard hats, and safety shoes, goggles, gloves, hearing protection and respirators. OSHA's primary personal protective equipment standards are in Title 29 of the Code of Federal Regulations (CFR), Part 1910 General Industry Standards. ASP's will conduct a hazard assessment of the workplace to determine what hazards are present that require the use of protective equipment, provide workers with appropriate
protective equipment, provide training, require workers to use PPE and maintain it in sanitary and reliable condition.

Using personal protective equipment is generally the last line of defense after engineering controls, work practices, and administrative controls are in place. Engineering controls involve physically changing a machine or work environment. Administrative controls involve changing how or when workers do their jobs, such as scheduling work and rotating workers to reduce exposures. Work practices involve training workers how to perform tasks in ways that reduce their exposure to workplace hazards.

Knowledge Areas

1. Assessment of need for personal protective equipment

OSHA standard 29 CFR 1910.132 requires employers to assess the workplace to determine if hazards are present, or are likely to be present, which necessitate the use of PPE employers must institute all feasible engineering and work practice controls to eliminate and reduce hazards before using PPE to protect against hazards

This requires the ASP to survey each work area and job or task. Review the hazards to which employees may be exposed while performing the work activities or while present in the work area. Determine control of the hazards consisting of engineering, work place, and/or administrative controls to eliminate or reduce the hazards before resorting to using PPE.

2. Selection and testing of personal protective equipment

The workplace survey identifies sources of hazards to feet, head, eyes and face of workers. Reassess whenever a new hazard is introduced into the workplace. Adequate protection against the highest level of each of the hazards should be provided. Care should be taken to recognize the possibility of multiple and simultaneous exposure to a variety of hazards.

Selection of PPE is based on:

- **Sources of chemical exposures.**
- **Sources of hazardous atmospheres.**
- **Sources of impact or motion** such as machinery or processes where any movement of tools, machine elements or particles could exist or movement of personnel that could result in collision with stationary objects.
- **Sources of high temperatures** that could result in burns, eye injury or ignition of protective equipment.

- **Sources of hazardous radiation** such as welding, brazing, cutting, furnaces, heat treating, high intensity lights.
- **Sources of falling objects** or potential for dropping objects.
- **Sources of sharp objects** which might pierce the feet or cut hands.
- **Sources of rolling or pinching objects** which could crush the feet.

Select PPE which ensures a level of protection greater than the minimum required to protect employees from the hazards. PPE that fits well and is comfortable to wear will encourage employee use.

Fit the device. If PPE does not fit properly it may not provide the level of protection desired and may discourage employee use. Reassess hazards when new equipment or processes introduce hazards that might require revised PPE strategies.

3. Usage of personal protective equipment

Employers are required to train each employee who must use PPE. Employees must be trained to know the following:

- When PPE is necessary.
- What PPE is required.
- How to properly use, don and doff adjust and wear the PPE.
- The limitations of the PPE.
- Proper care, maintenance, the useful life and disposal of PPE.

The ASP must ensure each employee **demonstrates** an understanding of the PPE training as well as the ability to properly wear and use PPE **before** they are allowed to perform work requiring the use of PPE. If the ASP determines a previously trained employee is not demonstrating the proper understanding and skill level in the use of PPE the employee should receive **retraining**. Training must be documented.

4. Maintenance of personal protective equipment

PPE must be kept clean and sanitary. Maintain PPE in accordance with manufacturer's instructions. Some PPE may require special cleaning, in these cases use the manufacturer's recommendations. If PPE is contaminated and cannot be decontaminated safely, it may need disposed of in a special manner to protect other employees from exposure to the hazard. PPE shall be stored in such a way that it will not become contaminated such as plastic bags, lockers, closets, or drawers. PPE is not to be used if it is damaged and in need of repair. Be cognizant of ANSI Z87.1-2003 PPE Standards.

The ASP must know the requirements for a PPE inspection program.

• Inspection and operational testing of equipment received as new from manufacturer or distributor.
• Inspection of equipment as it is selected for a particular operation.
• Inspection of equipment after use or training and prior to maintenance.
• Periodic inspection of stored equipment for shelf life.

Prior to use:
- Determine that the material is correct for the specified task at hand.
- Hold up to light and check for pinholes – Flex product: look for cracks and other signs of
Deterioration.
- Visually inspect for imperfect seams, non-uniform coatings, tears and malfunctioning closures.
- If the product has been used previously, inspect inside and out for signs of chemical degradation, discoloration, swelling, or stiffness.

During use periodically inspect for:

• Evidence of chemical degradation such as discoloration, swelling, stiffening and softening tears, punctures, or cracks.

Safety Fundamentals Examination Domain 3

Safety, Health, and Environmental Training and Management 20.6%

Topic 1 - Training and Communication Methods

Safety training methods cover needs analysis, performance objectives, instructional strategy and methods, content, delivery evaluation and costs. ASP's will develop performance-based training processes and identify training and non-training solutions.

1. Adult learning techniques

You need to know adult learners seek to build their self-esteem through practical learning activities in which their competency is enhanced. Adults have a strong need to be able to successfully apply what they learn to the job. If they think safety training is a waste of their time, they are not likely to be motivated to learn. Adult motivation occurs on four integrated and increasingly more effective levels.

- **Success** where the learner believes that he or she has the ability to successfully complete the training.
- **Volition** where the learner has a sense of choice or willingness to learn.
- **Value** where the learner thinks the training is important.
- **Enjoyment** where the learner not only feels confident about completing the training, they are willing and they believe it's important, they also have fun learning.

2. ANSI/ASSE Z490.1 (American National Standard: Criteria for Accepted Practices in Safety, Health, and Environmental Training)

You need to know the **ANSI Guidelines for evaluating training programs** ANSI Z490.1-2001 are the Accepted Practices in Safety Health and Environmental Training, which recommends evaluating three important elements of a safety training program.

Training program management indicates training works best when it's designed and implemented as an integrated system rather than a series of unrelated training sessions. Training should be evaluated to include:
- Responsibility, Authority, and Accountability
- Facilities and equipment
- Program Development
- Course Delivery
- Program Evaluation
- Documentation and records

The training process should be conducted using a systematic process that includes a needs assessment, objectives, course materials, lesson plans, evaluation strategies, and criteria for successful completion. This includes:
- Training goals
- Learning environment
- Adequacy of learning objectives
- Effectiveness of the training process

Training results should be evaluated to make improvements to existing plans and gain awareness of the need for new training. Items that should be evaluated include:
- The training action-plan
- Long-term strategic planning
- Needs assessment
- Prioritizing training
- Adequate support and funding

3. Behavior modification

Behavior-Based Safety is a process that helps employees identify and choose a safe behavior over an unsafe one. Behavior-based safety is based on four key components:
- A behavioral observation and feedback process.
- A formal review of observation data.
- Improvement goals.
- Reinforcement for improvement and goal attainment.

Behavior modification helps reduce losses organizations experience from accidents. Reducing accidents and lost-time injuries through a rewards may be a goal. An effective safety incentive program defines objectives, sets goals, plans and assigns responsibility and accountability, and implements and manages the program goals.

Safety committees play a key role in the safety program as they normally consist of elected or voluntary employees from various departments. The main function of a safety committee is to create and maintain interest in safety and health, thereby helping to reduce accidents.

4. Methods of training delivery

OSHA Guidelines for Instructor Competency define a "Competent" as possessing the skills, knowledge, experience, and judgment to perform assigned tasks or activities satisfactorily as determined by the employer. Instructors should be deemed competent on the basis of previous documented experience in their area of instruction, successful completion of a train-the-trainer program specific to the topics they will teach, and an evaluation of instructional competence.

Trainers should be able to demonstrate an appropriate level of technical knowledge, skills, or abilities in the subjects they teach. Trainers should be able to demonstrate adequate competency in delivery techniques and methods appropriate to adult learning. The methods used for training include hands on, paper, audio, presentation, classroom, and online computer based.

5. Methods of training evaluation

The level of evaluation measures both the learner and immediate safety culture. It gauges how well the learner applied the training. For training to be truly effective, the safety culture must support the training by preventing, discouraging, encouraging and requiring. The methods for evaluating training are before and after comparisons, questionnaires, and interviews. Best practices:

- Measure behaviors against standards developed by a control group.
- Allow enough time after training to make sure behaviors have been incorporated.
- Observe students, interview supervisors/coworkers.
- Sample an appropriate percentage of trainees.
- Sample all trainees if appropriate.

6. Presentation tools

Presentation tools may include audience training, one on one, visual and audio for general safety education and specific safety training on performing safe procedures and practices.

Topic 2 - Management Processes

1. Emergency/crisis/disaster planning and response

You need to know when developing an emergency response plan a risk assessment should be conducted to identify potential emergency scenarios. The emergency plan should be consistent with your performance objectives. The ASP should develop or be involve in the emergency plan development for protecting employees, visitors, contractors and anyone else in the workplace. Emergency and crisis planning should include protective actions for life safety including building evacuation, fire drills, sheltering from severe weather such as tornadoes, shelter-in-place and possible lockdown.

2. Identification of expert resources

Expert resources may be required if a process review, accident investigation, or chemical industrial hygiene knowledge need exceeds the knowledge base or licensing requirement of an ASP such as a resident engineer RE.

3. Incident data collection and analysis

Incidence rates can be used to show the relative level of injuries and illnesses among different industries, firms, or operations. These rates can help determine both problem areas and progress in preventing work-related injuries and illnesses. The Bureau of Labor Statistics (BLS) has developed these instructions to provide a step by step approach for employers to evaluate their firm's injury and illness record. Data typically includes the number of nonfatal injuries and illnesses based on the number of hours all employees actually worked.

4. Techniques for performing incident investigation and root cause analysis

You need to know timely and accurate reporting allows for the ASP to understand patterns, discover contributing factors, identification of risks, reduction of loss, and reduction of mishaps. The purpose of accident investigation is to locate and define procedural errors and hazards which contributed to the accident. This includes: determining causal factors, fact finding, documentation of findings, and management involvement.

Topic 3 - Inspections and Auditing

Inspections and audits should be routine in frequency and are used to identify risks in advance. This enables identification of employees at risk of exposure and effectiveness of countermeasures establishment of a baseline for continuous processes, and the current state of housekeeping in the organization.

1. Elements of an inspection and auditing program

Inspections and audits should give equal consideration to accident, fire, and environmental health
exposures, storage of incompatibles, explosives, and other hazard situations.

Inspections will include effective safety observation, determining technical problems, chemical compatibility inspections, condemning equipment and making recommendations for building conditions, cryogenic safety, emergency evacuation, employer posting, fire protection, procedures such as LOTO, and waste accumulation.

2. Reasons to perform inspections and audits

Safety inspections are a basic tool for establishing and maintaining safe conditions and discovering unsafe practices in the workplace. Systematic inspections are practical ways to identify and correct unsafe equipment, conditions, processes, and work practices. If unsafe conditions and practices are found to exist prompt corrective actions are can be initiated.

The ASP will observe work practices, search for hidden hazards - do not accept initial impressions, guard against habit and familiarity pitfalls, record observations systematically and use a checklist.

3. Purpose and objective of ISO 19011 (Guidelines for quality and/or environmental management systems auditing)

ISO 19011 provides guidance on the principles of auditing, managing audit programs, conducting quality management system audits and environmental management system audits, as well as guidance on the competence of quality and environmental management system auditors. It is applicable to all organizations needing to conduct internal or external audits of quality and/or environmental management systems or to manage an audit program.

Topic 4 - Group Dynamics

Group dynamics refers to the attitudinal and behavioral characteristics of a group. Group dynamics concern how groups form, their structure and process, and how they function. Group performance varies depending on enthusiasm level and commitment towards a goal. Group dynamic is influenced by the individual needs in relation to Maslow's Hierarchy of needs. Motivators of groups include recognition, achievement, advancement, and the work itself.

1. Conflict resolution

You need to know the process for managing conflict involves the following steps. 1. Prepare for conflict as it is inevitable in most projects. 2. Acknowledge conflict and address it as it occurs. 3. Manage appropriate conflict response and implement it. Responses to conflict may include forcing, avoiding, accommodating, collaborating, and compromise. Methods for resolving conflict include mediation, arbitration, control, acceptance, and elimination.

As conflict is inevitable on projects so is change. Change often causes stress in individuals. The ASP must monitor the cycle of change for potential intervention as conflict and stress may be self-perpetuating.

2. Methods of facilitating teams

Facilitation of teams requires understanding of behavioral tendencies, biases, preferred modes of communication, motivation, and decision making. Leadership of the team includes directing, coaching, supporting, and delegating.

3. Multidisciplinary teamwork

Multidisciplinary teams will produce the best results because of the cross functional representation and expertise. Teamwork will evolve through four stages of forming, storming, norming, and performing. In stage 1 forming, there is high dependence on a leader for guidance and direction. In stage 2, storming team members vie for position as they attempt to establish themselves in relation to other team members and the leader. In stage 3 norming, agreement and consensus largely forms among the team, who respond well to facilitation by leader. Roles and responsibilities are clear and accepted. In stage 4 performing, the team is more strategically aware and knows clearly why it is doing what it is doing. The team has a shared vision.

4. Negotiation procedures

You need to know negotiation is a process that is predicated on a manager's ability to use influence productively. Insist on using objective criteria, objective data, and measurable criteria form the best basis for accurate negotiations. Develop fair standards and procedures requiring both parties to negotiate from the same basic understanding of the terms and liabilities.

Topic 5 - Project Management

Knowledge Areas

1. Evaluation of cost, schedule, performance, and risk

Projects will typically be managed with a work breakdown structure which reflects the way a project will be planned, cost estimated, and managed. Cost estimated and cost budgets will be managed for resourcing the project. Cost estimating techniques include analogous – top down approach, parametric – modeled from history, and bottom up – team involvement. Scheduling is based on effort and duration. Performance is measured and controlled through collection of actual versus forecasted, actual to plan, and variance to impact. Risk management includes identifying risks, evaluating the importance, prioritizing the risks, developing risk tolerance, and managing those above the threshold.

2. Project management terminology

Project management terminology can be quite extensive the most important terms include:

Critical Path Method which includes the sequence of events and the duration of a project. **Project Scope** includes the sum of products services and results to be provided as a project.

Work Breakdown Structure (WBS) is the deliverable oriented hierarchical decomposition of the work to be executed by a project team to accomplish project objectives.

3. Review of specifications and designs against requirements

Review of specifications and designs against requirements requires reviewing functional requirement specifications which describe the detailed functionality of the equipment or design. It is usually developed by the supplier. Configuration management and change control documentation is the formal process by which qualified representatives of appropriate disciplines review proposed or actual changes that might affect a validated and or approved status.

Topic 6 -Risk Management

Knowledge Areas

1. The risk management process

You need to know risk management is a four step process. The step are:

> **1. Risk identification** - which is the process of determining the specific risk factors that can reasonably be expected to affect your project.
>
> **2. Analysis of probability and consequences** – which are the potential impact of these risk factors, determined by how likely they are to occur and the effect they would have on the project if they did occur.
>
> **3. Risk mitigation strategies** – are the steps taken to minimize the potential impact of those risk factors deemed sufficiently threatening to a project.
>
> **4. Control and documentation** – creates a knowledgebase for future projects based on lessons learned.

2. Risk analysis methods (e.g., job safety analysis, hazard and operability analysis, failure mode and effects analysis, fault tree analysis, whatif/ checklist analysis, change analysis)

A Job Safety Analysis (JSA) is a method that can be used to identify, analyze and record the steps involved in performing a specific job, the existing or potential safety and health hazards associated with each step, and the recommended action(s) or procedure(s) that will eliminate or reduce these hazards and the risk of a workplace injury or illness.

Hazard and Operability Analysis (HAZOP) is a reputable and well proven method for identifying safety and operational issues related to the design, operation and maintenance of a process system. It involves systematic examination as a multidisciplinary study involving human errors, led by an independent person.

Failure Modes and Effects Analysis (FMEA) is a systematic, proactive method for evaluating a process to identify where and how it might fail and to assess the relative impact of different failures, in order to identify the parts of the process that are most in need of change. FMEA includes review of the following:

- Failure modes - (What could go wrong?)
- Failure causes - (Why would the failure happen?)
- Failure effects - (What would be the consequences of each failure?)
- Steps in the process

Fault Tree Analysis – Is a technique that is used to identify the possible outcomes given the occurrence of an initiating event (or given event). A fault tree analysis (FTA) analyzes high-level failures and identifies all lower-level (sub-system) failures that cause it. The undesired event constitutes the highest level (top) event in a fault tree diagram and represents a complete or catastrophic failure of the system.

The What - if Checklist is a hazard assessment technique that combines the creative thinking of a selected team of specialists with the methodical focus of a prepared checklist. The team develops a comprehensive process hazards analysis that used in training operating personnel on the hazards of the particular operation.

Change Analysis should be performed whenever a significant modification or addition is made to the process. A team of operators, engineers, and safety and health professionals jointly analyze potential changes or new equipment before they are put online and identify safety and production concerns up front before problems develop.

Topic 7 - Safety, Health, and Environmental Management Systems

Knowledge Areas

1. Purpose and objective of ANSI/AIHA Z10 (American National Standard for Occupational Health and Safety Management Systems)

You need to know ANSI/AIHA Z10 (American National Standard for Occupational Health and Safety Management Systems) is the current blueprint for a better safety and health program which bridges the gap between what is required and what is suggested as a best practice. The standard is non-mandatory but serves as a benchmark for health and safety in productivity, financial performance, and quality. It also establishes a system to prevent lost time and lost resources due to worker injuries.

The standard has five elements

- Management leadership and employee participation
- Planning
- Implementation and operation
- Evaluation and corrective action
- Management review

2. Purpose and objective of the ISO 14000 series of environmental management system standards.

The ISO 14000 is series of voluntary standards relating to environmental management systems (EMS) and others which are tools to help companies develop environmental policy, develop objectives and targets, conduct environmental auditing, and evaluate environmental performance. This includes:

- Reduced raw material/resource use.
- Reduced energy consumption.
- Improved process efficiency.
- Reduced waste generation and disposal costs.
- Utilization of recoverable or recycled resources.

3. Purpose and objective of the OHSAS 18000 series of occupational health and safety management system standards

OHSAS 18001 is the internationally recognized assessment specification for occupational health and safety management systems. It was developed by a selection of leading trade bodies, international standards and certification bodies to address a gap where no third-party certifiable international standard exists. Services include:

•Planning for hazard identification, risk assessment and risk control
•OHSAS management program
•Structure and responsibility
•Training, awareness and competence
•Consultation and communication
•Operational control
•Emergency preparedness and response
•Performance measuring, monitoring and improvement

4. Purpose and objective of the U.S. Occupational Safety

The Occupational Safety and Health Administration (OSHA) was established by the Williams-Steiger Occupational Safety and Health Act (OSH Act) of 1970. OSHA's mission is to ensure that every working man and woman in the nation is employed under safe and healthful working conditions. OSHA is an administrative agency within the United States Department of Labor and administered by an assistant secretary of labor.

OSHA seeks to make workplaces safer and healthier by making and enforcing regulations called standards in the OSH Act. The Act itself establishes only one workplace standard, which is called the "general duty standard." The general duty standard states: "Each employer shall furnish to each of his employees employment and a place of employment which are free from recognized hazards that are causing or are likely to cause death or serious physical harm to his employees." Standards made by OSHA are published in the Code of Federal Regulations (CFR).

OSHA requires all companies subject to its workplace standards to abide by a variety of occupational regulations. All employers covered by the OSH Act are required to keep four kinds of records:
- Records regarding enforcement of OSHA standards
- Research records
- Job-related injury, illness, and death records
- Job hazard records

Safety Fundamentals Examination Domain 4

Business Principles, Practices, and Metrics in Safety, Health, and Environmental Practice

13.1%

Topic 1 - Basic Financial Principles

Knowledge Areas

1. Cost benefit analysis (e.g., calculating, evaluating, and selecting the best alternative)

You need to know a cost benefit analysis is the process of quantifying costs and benefits of a decision, program, or project over a period of time and those of its alternatives within the same period in order to have a single scale of comparison for unbiased evaluation. The CBA is not limited to monetary considerations only. It often includes environmental and social costs and benefits that can be reasonably quantified. In the case of the ASP cost benefits analysis are often performed in comparison of accident and injury rates to equipment and engineering control costs.

2. Definition and use of life cycle cost

You need to know life cycle costs are the sum of all recurring and one-time (non-recurring) costs over the full life span or a specified period. Life cycle costs impact organizational operational costs and the life cycle costs of safety programs must be monitored and not avoided. ASP's may be required to develop the cost of a safety process, feature, or piece of equipment over the life of its use.

3. Definition and use of net present value

You need to know net present value (NPV) is the difference between the present value of the future cash flows from an investment and the amount of investment. Present value of the expected cash flows is computed by discounting them at the required rate of return.

Net present value is the most popular financial decision making approach in project selection. The computed values include net cash flow for a period, the required rate of return, initial cash investment, and inflation rate for the period.

4. Definition and use of return on investment

Return on investment is a measure of profitability that indicates whether or not a company is using its resources in an efficient manner. It is also referred to as rate of return or yield for a project. Return on investment is a measure of the amount gained or lost on an investment expressed as a percentage of the initial investment. The formula for calculating ROI is Final Value of Investment - Initial Value of Investment / Initial Value of Investment.

Topic 2 -Probability and Statistics

The ASP may be required to perform a probability-based safety analysis mathematically determining risk based on the number of occurrences of an accident in proportion to the population base such as code safety factor decisions and optimum design where the objective includes safety and cost.

1. Concepts of probability

Probability is the chance that something will happen or how likely it is that some event will happen. This can be outcomes and events as an odd or even percentage, outcome of events where if A happens and B happens the overlapping of A and B may cause C or Conditional probability which states if one event occurs another event may occur as a result of it.

2. Normal (Gaussian) distribution: description, calculations, and Interpretations

Normal distribution is also called Gaussian distribution and because of its curved flaring shape may be referred to as the "bell curve." The normal distribution as an approximation to the binomial distribution and is used to study measurement errors. The standard normal distribution is given by taking mu=0 and sigma^2=1 in a general normal distribution. The normal distribution curve allows safety professionals to visualize how far out of the normal distribution an accident or failure process is out of the norm. This picture depicts a normal distribution curve. Normal distributions are symmetrical, bell-shaped distributions that are useful in describing real-world data. The *standard* normal distribution, represented by the letter Z, is the normal distribution having a mean of 0 and a standard deviation of 1.

3. Poisson distribution: description, calculations, and interpretations

Poisson distribution is one of the discrete probability distribution. It is used for calculating the possibilities for an event such as an accident with the given average rate of value(λ). A poisson random variable(x) refers to the number of success in a poisson experiment. Recognize the formula: of f(x) = e-λλx / x!   where:

λ is an average rate of value.
x is a poisson random variable.
e is the base of logarithm(e=2.718).

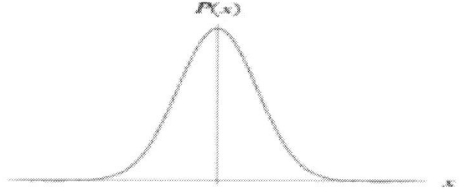

$$f(k; \lambda) = \frac{\lambda^k e^{-\lambda}}{k!}$$

4. Descriptive statistics: description, calculations, and interpretations (e.g., mean, mode, median, standard deviation, standard error of measurement, variance)

The ASP will be required to manipulate and understand data of the mean, mode, median, standard deviation, standard error of measurement, and variance. The Mean is an average of the total fond by adding all of the numbers in the set and divided by the number in the list. The Median is found by listing numbers arranged in order from lowest to highest. The number in the middle or the average of the two middle numbers is the median. The Mode refers to the number in a list that occurs most often. Standard deviation is the variance in measure that a data point deviates from the norm. The error of measurement is the probability of error in a measurement system.

5. Inferential statistics: description, calculations, and interpretations (e.g., ttest, z-test, chi-square test, Pearson product-moment correlation, Spearman's rank correlation, linear regression techniques, confidence intervals, control limits)

Inferential statistics are required in analysis of safety processes. They are mathematical methods that employ probability theory for deducing (inferring) the properties of a population from the analysis of the properties of a data sample drawn from it. Inferential statistics determine the precision and reliability of the inferences it helps to draw.

Topic 3 - Performance Metrics and Indicators

Knowledge Areas

1. Lagging indicators (e.g., incidence rates, lost time, direct costs of incidents)

Lagging indicator: is an indicator that follows an event (e.g. rate of incidents and injuries).

Lagging indicators measures facts about past events. Examples of lagging measures include:

- OSHA citations by number of citations and type
- Workers' compensation claim trends and amounts
- Lost workday rate
- Injury frequency and severity
- Fatality or other accidents
- Chemical releases
- Experience modification rate
- Near misses in frequency and by trend

2. Leading indicators (e.g., inspection frequency, number of safety interventions, employee performance evaluations, training frequency, near miss/near hit reporting)

The ASP will need to know a leading indicator is an indicator that signals future events or positive efforts towards preventing injury and illness such as inspections completed and use of safe work practices. Leading indicators focus on future performance. Examples of leading indicators include:

- The number of inspections or audits performed in a given time frame.
- The number of work orders or accident investigations performed on time.

- The percentage of safe behaviors observed in the workplace.
- The percentage of personal protective equipment (PPE) compliance.
- The number of "near miss" incidents reported and addressed.
- The percentage of on-time closure of safety inspection and audit findings.
- The number of health and safety training hours by job or risk classification.

3. Economic effects of losses (e.g., cost per incident)

Workplace injuries and illnesses have a major impact on a company's financial cost. It has been estimated that employers pay almost $1 billion per week for direct workers' compensation costs alone. The costs of workplace injuries and illnesses include direct and indirect costs. Direct costs include workers' compensation payments, medical expenses, and costs for legal services. Indirect costs include training replacement employees, accident investigation and implementation of corrective measures, lost productivity, repairs of damaged equipment and property, and costs associated with lower employee morale and absenteeism

- To calculate the number of accidents and recordable incidents retrieve data from the OSHA 300 log.
- Determine total the number of hours worked by all employees during the year including overtime hours, but not include vacation, paid sick leave or holiday pay.
- Multiply the number of recordable incidents by 200,000. The 200,000 represents how many hours would be worked by 100 employees, each putting in 40 hours per week over 50 weeks in a year; OSHA requires the accident rate to be expressed as incidents per 100 employees with maximum straight-time hours.
- Divide by the result by the total number of hours worked.

4. Relationship between cost of losses and the effect on profitability

You need to know the impact of accident costs on businesses. Key Statistics estimate direct U.S. workers compensation costs annually in the US are approximately $50 billion.

Each time an accident occurs the cost of the injury must be subtracted from profits. Direct costs are medical care for the employee. At a 5 percent profit margin an extra $20,000 in income is needed to compensate for a $1,000 injury. If the profit margin is near 1 percent, an additional $100,000 worth of new income is necessary to maintain that profit level for the same injury.

Indirect costs include, but are not limited to:

- Training or replacement worker including recruiting and training of a temporary or permanent worker.
- Costs for installing additional equipment safeguards or implementing new safety programs, including any regulatory compliance fines that may have resulted from an accident.
- Extra costs of employees overtime to make up lost production resulting from an accident.
- Management and administrative personnel time to complete accident investigation, report injury to insurance company and/or regulatory agencies, document accident logs and provide basic injury management involving employee follow-up.

Tips for the test

A good strategy some testers use is to review what you would also test for as a CSP which are available in the CSP guide on the BSCP website. It will be your next step in the certification and many of the information foundation is built on your daily safety professional activities. Having the level of knowledge for the next certification step is always an advantage in testing for the initial certification level.

Remember the ASP examination is an objective assessment of your foundation of knowledge and skills.

Make a checklist of topics that are concerning you as you near test time. Some of the questions will be mathematical in nature. Ensure you have not made simple mathematical errors.

Be cautious sometimes the answers that "sound" correct are incorrect based on the structure of the sentences by the test writer. Some of the answers are set for failure based on wording alone.

Sometimes new information in the answer response not included in the original question many times is an incorrect answer.

Skip the questions which have overly technical terms and return later to avoid time drain on your overall test.

20 Practice questions for the Associate Safety Professional Certification Exam

1. The main reason safety management programs fail is?

    a. Organizational emphasis is placed on activity oriented elements.

    b. Organization managers ignore basic management techniques

    c. Management fails to clearly define goals.

    d. a and b

2. What is the standard deviation of the following dataset of monthly injuries: 14, 17, 29, 34, 21?

    a. 9.42

    b. 8.33

    c. 3.43

    d. 5.82

3. Which of the following terms describes the maximum allowed OSHA exposure for workers during an 8 hour workday or 40 hour workweek?

    a. Exposure limit

    b. Ceiling limit

    c. Short term exposure limit (STEL)

    d. Permissible exposure limit (PEL)

4. A black cartridge on a respirator would protect against?

    a. Acid gas

    b. Organic Vapors

    c. Radioactive Material

    d. Dust and Mists

5. Compressed gas cylinders should never be exposed to temperatures greater than?

    a. 200 degrees Fahrenheit

    b. 125 degrees Fahrenheit

    c. 100 degrees Fahrenheit

    d. 150 degrees Fahrenheit

6. Class A fire protection and extinguishing systems must have a travel distance of no more than _____ feet?

    a. 75

    b. 100

    c. 25

    d. 50

7. To be classified as flammable a liquid must have a flashpoint which is:

    a. above 200 degrees Fahrenheit

    b. below 200 degrees Fahrenheit

    c. above 100 degrees Fahrenheit

    d. below 100 degrees Fahrenheit

8. Live parts of electrical equipment which operates at _____ volts or higher must be guarded against accidental contact.

    a. 100

    b. 120

    c. 24

    d. 50

9. A local chemical effect refers to an adverse health effect that takes place at the point or area of contact caused by what?

    a. a chemical that injures the skin, eyes, or respiratory system

    b. repeated exposure to a chemical

    c. a single exposure to a chemical

    d. only teratogenic compounds

10. Displaying accident rate data to organizational management is best reflected by the use of what diagram?

    a. Cause and effect Ishikawa diagram

    b. Process flow diagram

    c. Histogram

    d. Failure modes and effects analysis (FMEA)

11. Project management methods to determine risk management strategies requires a quantitative analysis of impact and probability. The formula for a quantitative analysis of probability, impact and expected value is?

    a. $EV = P \times I$

    b. $PI = 2EV$

    c. $EV = 2prv$

    d. $2r - 3EV = P$

12. Which is the correct definition of expected value?

    a. Frequency times impact of risk.

    b. Probability times impact of a risk.

    c. Rate of return based on change.

    d. Value based on change.

13. Which of the following instructional techniques is most effective for decontamination training?

    a. Demonstration hands on technique

    b. Information sheet

    c. Visual aid

    d. quiz

14. General Industry Standards 1910 require a guardrail be at minimum _____ inches to protect the greatest number of people from falling?

    a. 32 inches

    b. 36 inches

    c. 40 inches

    d. 42 inches

15. A commonly reported problem associated with tingling, pain, or numbness in the thumb and first three fingers is referred to as:

    a. Asperger's syndrome

    b. Carpel tunnel syndrome

    c. Trigger finger

    d. Raynaud's syndrome

16. Airborne concentrations of hydrocarbons are expressed in what unit of measure?

    a. STEL

    b. mg/m3

    c. kg/m2

    d. ppm

17. What is the OSHA exposure limit for formaldehyde based on an 8 hour TWA?

    a. .82 ppm

    b. .75 ppm

    c. 1.0 ppm

    d. 11 ppm

18. The quantity of radiation absorbed per unit mass is a dose expressed in what?

    a. microcuries

    b. radioisotopes

    c. minicuries

    d. roentgens and rems

19. OSHA requires safety belt and lanyard hardware used in fall arrest systems to withstand a tensile load of how much in pounds?

    a. 4000

    b. 2000

    c. 3800

    d. 2200

20. An exposure monitoring and medical surveillance program must be in place for what level of ethylene oxide exposure?

    a. 2.0 ppm

    b. 1.0 ppm

    c. 0.5 ppm

    d. 0.025 ppm

Correct Answers

1. The correct answer is (d.) The main reason safety management programs fail is that organizational emphasis is placed on activity oriented elements and organization managers ignore basic management techniques.

2. The correct answer is (b.) The standard deviation of the following dataset of monthly injuries: 14, 17, 29, 34, 21 is 8.33.

3. The correct answer is (d) The term which describes the maximum allowed OSHA exposure for workers during an 8 hour workday or 40 hour workweek is Permissible exposure limit (PEL). The Short term exposure limit (STEL) is the 15-min time weighted average exposure that should not be exceeded at any time during a workday even if the 8 hour time weighted average is within the threshold limit value. The Ceiling limit is the absolute exposure limit that should not be exceeded at any time.

4. The correct answer is (b) A black cartridge on a respirator would protect against organic vapors. Acid gas cartridges are white, radioactive material cartridges are purple and dust and mists are orange.

5. The correct answer is (b) Compressed gas cylinders should never be exposed to temperatures greater than 125 degrees Fahrenheit.

6. The correct answer is (a) Class A fire protection and extinguishing systems must have a travel distance of no more than 75 feet.

7. The correct answer is (d) To be classified as flammable a liquid must have a flashpoint which below 100 degrees Fahrenheit.

8. The correct answer is (d) Live parts of electrical equipment which operates at 50 volts or higher must be guarded against accidental contact.

9. The correct answer is (a) A local chemical effect refers to an adverse health effect that takes place at the point or area of contact caused by what a chemical that injures the skin, eyes, or respiratory system.

10. The correct answer is (c) Displaying accident rate data to organizational management is best reflected by the use of a histogram displayed by accident category or trend.

11. The correct answer is (a) Project management methods to determine risk management strategies requires a quantitative analysis of impact and probability. The formula for a quantitative analysis of probability, impact and expected value is EV=P x I. The remaining answers were fabricated.

12. The correct answer is (b) The correct definition of expected value is probability times impact of a risk.

13. The correct answer is (a) Demonstration hands on instructional technique is most effective for decontamination training.

14. The correct answer is (d) General Industry Standards 1910 require a guardrail be at minimum 42 inches to protect the greatest number of people from falling.

15. The correct answer is (b) A commonly reported problem associated with tingling, pain, or numbness in the thumb and first three fingers is referred to as carpel tunnel syndrome.

16. The correct answer is (b) Airborne concentrations of hydrocarbons are expressed in mg/m3 unit of measure.

17. The correct answer is (b) The OSHA exposure limit for formaldehyde based on an 8 hour TWA is .75 ppm.

18. The correct answer is (d) The quantity of radiation absorbed per unit mass is a dose expressed in what roentgens and rems.

19. The correct answer is (a) OSHA requires safety belt and lanyard hardware used in fall arrest systems to withstand a tensile load of 4000 pounds.

20. The correct answer is (c) An exposure monitoring and medical surveillance program must be in place for o.5 ppm level of ethylene oxide exposure.

Made in the USA
Columbia, SC
13 January 2018